ERRATICS

CATHY BRYANT

ARACHNE PRESS

First published in UK 2018 by Arachne Press Limited
100 Grierson Road, London SE23 1NX
www.arachnepress.com
© Arachne Press 2018
ISBN: 978-1-909208-56-8

The moral rights of the author have been asserted
All content is copyright the author.

All rights reserved. This book is sold subject to the condition that it shall not by way of trade or otherwise, be lent, resold, hired out or otherwise circulated without the publisher's prior written consent in any form or binding or cover other than that in which it is published and without similar condition including this condition being imposed on the subsequent purchaser.
Except for short passages for review purposes no part of this publication may be reproduced, stored in a retrieval system or transmitted in any form, or by any means, electronic, mechanical, photocopying, recording or otherwise without prior written permission of Arachne Press.

Poems collected here previously appeared in
Contemporary Verse 2, The Sunlight Press, Balticon 49, *Stairs and Whispers* (Nine Arches 2017), The Scarlet Leaf Review ,Star Line,
Eye to the Telescope, Antarctica Journal, WaxPoetryArt , Prole, Calculated was first published by The Science Fiction and Fantasy Poetry Association, The Curly Mind, Polutexni, Stirred Feminist Collective,Silver Birch, The American Poetry Journal, Wordrunner Chapbooks
Printed on wood-free paper in the UK by TJ International, Padstow.

CONTENTS

Introduction	5
Flyleaves, Frontispieces, Dedications and Acknowledgments	6
Song of the Star Cleaners	7
Material	8
The Broken Column of the Truly Phallic	10
Circus	11
Stripped Ease	12
The Fish Who Saw Narcissus	13
The Huge Paws of Country Fog	14
As Dark Asda	15
Daffodils After the Zombie Apocalypse	16
Seeing the Glass as Half-full or Half-empty	17
January Joggers	18
How I Learned 'Welsh in a Week'	20
Erratics	23
Dear Sir/Madam/Darling	24
Secret Knowledge	25
Morecambe	26
Calculated	28
Going Beep in the Night	29
Not Cricket	30
Ms Bryant is Dangerously Delusional	32
Bite Down Hard	34
Cargo	35
Bardmon K's review of 'Poem' by A. Famous-Poet	36
Falconar's Flautist	37

Fear and the Familiar	38
I Have Tried to Stop Eating Stars	39
Social Etiquette, 1950s	40
Sylvia Plath Talks about England	41
Transition	42
Midnight Moments in the Mosh Pit (The Ted Hughes Rap)	43
Morphinesque	44
Shit People Say to Bisexuals	45
Wuthering, Wuthering, Wuthering Heights	46
There Must be Something In It	48
Skeleton Orchestra	49
Witness Statement	50
Aurora Borealis/ Migraine	51
You Might as Well Fuck	52
Still Life	54
Take Five Decades	55
Such Life and Brilliance	56
Warmer Places	57
Bloddeuwedd's Trinity	58
Such a Thing, My Leaping, Dancing Heart	59

Introduction

In the red corner: the muck, grit and harsh truths of life. In the blue corner: the beauty of the natural world and the vivid variety provided by imagination.
I'm dancing about somewhere in between.
To continue the boxing ring metaphor to a silly (but possibly accurate) degree, the other two corners are culture and experience, the canvas is time and I'm on the ropes of conscience.
For I'm stuck as a misfit. I was born in the south but I live in the north. I was born into the middle classes but I'm working class by poverty and experience. I know what it's like to be homeless, and what it's like to pick a dirty penny off the pavement and be happy to have it, and I also know the correct way to address a duchess, and whether to put the milk in first (Your Grace, unless you're a duchess too; and don't, ever). I don't fit in anywhere – except at poetry events, where you can't know whether the person next to you is a convicted felon, a linguistics professor, or both.
I first saw erratics – rocks and stones moved to odd places by long-gone glaciers – at Greenfields in North Manchester, where the title poem is set. Like the black knives of cypresses in the otherwise bright Mediterranean, the standing stones look strange, and jar the system, yet are absolutely right too. The countryside, urban life, and poetry are all full of the unexpected in the same way. This is how I feel, now, about misfits and oddities. I've come far from the teenager who wished that she could fit in. This collection celebrates the offbeat, the unfashionable, the playful and the strange.

Flyleaves, Frontispieces, Dedications and Acknowledgments

To Dear, Dearest, Miss, Mr, Mrs, Honourable,
Lady, His Royal Highness, the delightful, the most.
All errors. All errors are.

Frontispiece Illustration: *She crept along the dark passage.*

To my mother. To Doctor Freud.
The volume is respectful. Thanks are due.
My family, Rosamund Juliet Mark Joseph
Lin Salman Wendy Anthea Sita Jobeth Alice
volumes. Too many to mention here.

Frontispiece Illustration: *With misgivings, he entered the wood.*

With deepest profoundest sincerely felt.
My agent. My publishers. So grateful
for such helpful advice. All errors, all mistakes.
Far too many to mention. Thanks.
I have been lucky enough. To all those,
for their help and invaluable research.

Frontispiece Illustration: *The Author, aged 23, pen-and-ink.*
Caption: *Shortly before her death.*

All mistakes and errors will be attributed to me.
Reprinted fourteen times. Special edition. Classic.
Major motion picture starring the Author's Estate.
Foreword by errors. Classic. The Author acknowledges
the debts. All mistakes and errors are reproduced
without permission. Volumes. Posthumous. Thanks.

Songs of the Starcleaners

Long ago we swept huts, renewed the rushes
on the packed-earth floor. Then we wiped wood;
next stone.

In offices we learned to use miniature
vacuums on keyboards, special cloths
on monitors.

We sang our songs,
to which no one ever listened,
while we made everything fresher, nicer.

Later came the starships, and still
we were more cost-effective than robots.
So we sluiced spacesuits, dusted the bridge,
mopped the holodecks.

When the ultra-rich bought planets,
massive crews of us were flown in
to scrub the seas and tidy continents.
Generations of us lived and died there,
with our own culture, our own art.

Still no one ever listens to us
or our songs. And in ten thousand years,
when the casual owners of the future
survey what they own, they still
will not hear us, will be unable to see us,
however bright the shining light
from the stars we polish.

Material

I'm lying dozing in my room of cold stone in Tuscany,
window open to citrus breezes and the sizzle of cicadas,
when a bat flies in.
He – he is a he, I think blearily – lands on the bed,
hooks himself on, and we regard each other,
visitor bat and me.
Not the young vampire type, he would prefer a fine teacup
to a vein. Nor the big-eared wild-mouse opera sort
but a touch tubby round the middle;
probably a retired librarian.

Judging by my experience of bats,
which is confined to a school trip to a Lancashire mill
now turned museum – desperate that, turning into a museum
– now was it cotton or wool that they milled here, once?
Eh, no matter now which – in one room clinging to nothing
on a wall were tiny black umbrellas
that could have done with a dust.
A child, I longed to touch, but no – 'They're protected,'
hissed the guide proudly in her replica mob cap and shawl,
quite possibly knocked out in some sweatshop.

– judging by that –
the bat on my bed is clearly called Bernard.
We sit and take agreeable interest in each other,
with the silent courtesy and goodwill that are the best
of behaviours, caring nothing for species or voice.
He perches on my old-as-the-villa counterpane
(with the exquisite embroidery, all hand done)
and is resolutely unpredatory, as am I,
mindful of Lawrence so foolish with sticks and stones
and snakes and manliness, and that, for ten minutes or so,
is that.

Then Bernard apologises, takes his leave,
regrets he has another appointment; and I bow to him,
feel misery, loss, clumsy pettiness anyway,
imagining him out dining on fruit or wingèd things
or flying in soft star-pricked air while I lie here,
a great flabby lump of static humanity.
Yet he visited every night that I was there,
for this connection that declines to be named.
It's not lost, not gone. Just rare.

The Broken Column of the Truly Phallic

Why don't men refer to things as phallic that are floppy and disappointing?
Journeys to the Underworld, Fiona Pitt-Kethley, founder of International Penis Day.

The collapsed soggy newspaper.
The drooping corners of a disappointed mouth.
Slush that was a snowman yesterday.
The cake that failed to rise.
A plant gone brown and wilted.
Half-drunk coffee gone cold.

The interview that went badly;
the performance fallen flat.
The date who's only half there, mind glazed
and wandering, eyes vaguely on other possibilities.
The grade lower than you'd hoped.
The cream that has just turned.
A match that won't strike.
A dieter's meal. A smoker's gum.

The much-loved monument become rubble.
The conversation that needed to happen,
but didn't. The follow-up single.
The big game rained off. The goalless draw.
The joke that made no one laugh.
The poem rejected. The delayed flight.
The broken-down train. The stale doughnut.

The knowledge that you haven't given satisfaction,
though you've been told that it doesn't matter.
The tears and mulling over –
and the hope that springs eternal, or at least,
comes up the following night
– usually.

Circus

The lights go up on bad dreams of a stunt man, a stunned man
and silent people in black who might be ninjas or stagehands.
Roll up, roll up, do you have a light, mate? Smoke clears
to reveal the magician and his assistant breaking up,
sawing their relationship in half. The Ringmaster's dressed
for hunting, taking bets on the trapeze artist's survival,
and which animals will later be whipped and chained;
shades of the sex games the Strong Man plays with himself.
To make it more exciting there's no safety net. *Jump, jump*
the audience shouts to the bemused contortionist.
How? Which way? How high? Exit left pursued by
a bareback rider, bare, a bear, and a smell of things trapped
like mice in sawdust and the Big Top a cat,
a big top hat. Rabbits are pulled out, some dead.
We remember, with nostalgia, bread.

Stripped Ease

The almost faked woman stands on the rage
and lowly, one by one, regrooves
her retaining clothes; does an egestive dance,
blinding away against a soul.
The rowd of mean fear at her
and look forward to motionless foe jobs
and the wormless coffering of form young beasts.
You gut what you pilfer, they slay.

The Fish Who Saw Narcissus

He was a living statue, ripple-kissed,
golden in the bowl of our eyes.
Most boys made noises,
tried to catch us or threw stones,
then left. He lay gazing and we saw,
through very different eyes,
this perfect being, who, like us,
understood the importance of surfaces.
The nature of the surface can mean
life or death to a fish like me.
Then they took him away, our splendid boy,
and all there was, was another flower.

The Huge Paws of Country Fog

It hunts in packs, unseen until it roars
down the hillside, swallows you and kills you.

Today it ate us and the car and all
we could see was a fur of verge and grey
before us.

We did actually scream as oily paws
of panther-black fog tumbled over the road,
alive and young and fierce
against the immovable wall of paler mist.
It is unquestionably a living thing.

The car inched forward, terrified, crawling
– we had to speak in soothing voices,
then just touch it with the whip –
whimpering down Winnats Pass, glacier gorge,
to the hopeful village.

We knew it was there all the time,
the place of safety, with kettles
and lights and known roads.
Muffling our minds and scratching our eyes,
though, the fog does not go, not quite
and its feet are not small, but huge
and deadly, until the sunshine comes,
if it does.

As Dark Asda

Pirouetting up and down Asda aisles
in search of honeydew and harissa at half price,
I notice the changes.
A morose vampire baskets three tins of
Basics Blood for the week; a wolf
won't stop howling at the price of lean cuts.
A fairy with patched wings can't afford
her thimble of nectar and squarelet of gossamer;
her tears are swiftly harvested.
Two witches stand wondering just how on earth
they're supposed to make charms that open doors
to love and growth, when having to scrimp
– hoarding pinches of this, omitting a sprig of that.
I mean, it's bound to affect the efficacy.
The naiads can't afford bottles of clean water,
though the stromkarls sold their lutes.
I queue to face the pale wraiths
at the checkouts, along with muttering dwarves
and, miraculously, bright elves, unblemished
and unquenchable, sniffing their fresh baguettes
and treating themselves to a Twix, a Twirl and
some Tic Tacs. A sinister monk takes my card,
gives me worthless paper in return promising
jam savings tomorrow, and buy one nightmare
get one free. The wolf's at the door shaking
her charity tin, but the coins and amulets and
stones have lost their power. So many bills to pay,
so much hell to pay, and the netherworlds
are paying through the nose darkly.

Daffodils After the Zombie Apocalypse
(with apologies to William Wordsworth)

I zombied lonely as a cloud
that seeps down low o'er toxic hills
when all at once I saw a crowd,
a mob of ravaged daffodils;
beside the swamp, beneath dead trees,
cow'ring and sobbing in the breeze.

As patchy as the stars that wink
when moonlight shines on old barbed wire,
they barely made consistent link
along the scum-line of the mire;
doomed thousands merely dirty starch,
drooping heads in funeral march.

The murk beside them stank, but they
out-did the wastes in foul decay;
a poet could not but be prey
to melancholia today.
I stared and stared but little knew
the canker that would be my due.

For often, when alone I lie
in vacant or in pensive mood
they press down on that inward eye
that is the curse of solitude;
and then my heart with acid fills
and sickens with the daffodils.

Seeing the Glass as Half-full or Half-empty

There are many other possibilites.
The busy homeworker sees more washing up to do.
The cat sees something to knock over.
The lovers see something to share.
The conspiracy theorist sees that the water was drugged,
and the glass had a gun and was on the grassy knoll.
The racist believes that the glass will be stolen by immigrants.
The tv presenter sees (whether it's there or not) his reflection.
We depressives see something
that we'll no doubt drop, spill and break.
The musician flicks the note E. Ping!
The child sees a drink, or water for paintbrushes.
The surrealist sees that the glass is made of political bananas.

January Joggers

The better to display joggers' plumage, the days
are as grey as it gets. The first woman carries hot-pink weights
to match her top, trainers, headband, leggings and face;
that face is loaded with misery and boiling with embarassment.
She knows that she is drawing eyes, and she hates it all.
At least self-flagellation could be performed
in the comfort of one's own monastery.

Further on we drive past a perky ponytail,
its owner smiling, while behind lags her puffing boyfriend,
who has begun to hate her and her pert bottom.
He longs for warmth, fatty foods, soft flab.

Next is a man with sports drinks and headphones.
He has given up and sulk-walks, pug-faced with fractured pride,
his legs blue with cold; we can feel the goosepimples from here.
He is exposed, regretting his choice of little satin shorts.

The following week, like signs of allegiance to a rebel cause
or a secret society, bandages appear on ankle and knee,
and the odd elbow. The injured keep walking fiercely,
sometimes breaking into a wincing jog-lollop for a moment.
Their faces are slapped with their own defiance.
They still clutch accessories, their holy relics.

By February the season is over. All that can be spotted
are the regulars in their worn and comfortable gear
as they beat out a tattoo on their usual courses. They run
in the easy lope of healthy wolves, their minds roaming,
and for the first time we feel a touch of jealousy,
and more of admiration as we cough by in our fat cars.

How I Learned 'Welsh in a Week'

The buff-coloured pamphlet cost five new pence
in 1972. I was five, too, and excited
about the 'rapid' learning of 'conversational' Welsh.

Are you going to Wales?
Then I shall have the pleasure of your company.
Do we change carriages on the journey?
I should go to The Queen's Hotel if I were you.
You are very kind.

Six of us sardined in a tiny tin-can caravan.
It rained all week. We were surrounded
by surprisingly aggressive sheep.
We dreaded the muddy dash to the loos.

My luggage is at the station; please send for it.
Be so good as to bring me a fork.
I wish to have tea, with bread and butter
and cold meat. Give me notepaper,
envelopes, a pen and some ink.
Is there anything to be seen here?

One cold night we ran out of food
and put own-brand Weetabix in the toaster.
Marged, it was better than you'd expect.

There must have been shops and locals.
We bought food and souvenirs, I'm sure.
I must have spoken to real Welsh people.

Good morning, Sir! What can I show you?
I want a hat. A pair of stockings. Collars.
Is this the best you have?
We have some very good tea at half a crown.
I will take these. Please wrap them
and send them to The Queen's Hotel.

I know that we went out – we must have.
I remember a railway, and crying on a mountain,
fog and fern fighting my little legs;
but the caravan and the book
were the holiday and the event.

What! You here! Mary, call your mother.
I hope you are well. Are you a married man?
I should go to The Queen's Hotel if I were you.
I know him perfectly well.
Will you come for a walk?
Willingly. With great pleasure.
Make haste. I am waiting for you.
How far shall we go?

We left, driving sideways across the country,
like the rain.
Years later I went back,
minus book, family and caravan.
It wasn't the same. It was immeasurably better,
but far less memorable. Mary never did call her mother,
and no one, in any language, asked:

May I pluck a rose?
I must go.
Wait a little.
But really, I must go.
Remember me to all at home.
I hope to see you again soon.
Excuse my leaving you.
Farewell! a pleasant journey.

Hwyl fawr. Diolch.
(Thank you. Goodbye.)

Erratics

The hills and stones are drunker than us.
Someone spilled a thousand rolls of green velvet
at a party of rocks. We walk over them
and through the glissading stream with our
clompy boots and tupperware.

We're mushroom hunting on the fells.
It's like trying to spot a bird in a blizzard.
You have to tune in. There! Look!
Tiny freckles on the hill's skin.
We boil, fry, make tea to get them down.

Our stomachs fizz as new perceptions kick in.
Otherworld. More dimensions than usual,
but how many is usual? Can't remember.
There is no word in the world for that colour.
The standing stones are having a laugh.
New eyes open. We cry with pleasure
when the sun sets like concrete.

Later, someone is snoring Mendelssohn.
The stars are edible and slightly acidic.
The fire ambers then greys. In the morning
the miserable comedown is just the return
of normality, and the fact that the stones
have once more fallen silent, standing
sober and still.

Dear Sir/Madam/Darling

According to our records it is now six weeks
since I felt your tongue on my nipple,
or mine on yours. Please make arrangements
to make payment in full immediately,
either by direct debit or with roses and kisses.
It's hard to credit just how much one person
can ache for another under the circumstances,
contacting our accounts department for assistance.
Don't leave me waiting, with the possibility of
legal action, touching myself in installments.
Drizzle me with due and necessary sperm.
I must, must taste if you have paid the account
during the last few days, in which case please
ignore this letter. But you can't ignore our
undying passion for your convenience.
Yours sincerely, my beloved, In Flames
pp (signed on her behalf in her absence) x

Secret Knowledge

I know that the moon is made of chalk and cheese,
and smells of fresh apricots. By moonlight, cats dance,
twenty or thirty at a time, padding in silent circles
and weaving their tails in a complicated way.
It is best viewed from a low cloud or from the
uppermost branches of a yew tree, the sort that has
caches of rubies and old gold coins buried at its roots.
To find buried treasure sing a song in the key of D minor
about your mother, the moon and some cats,
accompanying yourself on the triangle or the rhombus.
Your mother knows all the secrets about triangles,
including the stuff that Euclid was too scared to share.
She can tell you which ones bite, and which can be
safely eaten. The safest thing in the world is the
olive, which is why Mediterranean people speak
happy river languages and live to the age of 223.
Rivers have voices, every last man jack of them.
Only the drowned can hear them and are greatly
comforted; but I have never been drowned so I have
never heard them. Therefore I cannot tell you any more.

Morecambe

There are no plants anywhere, unless you count cannabis smoke.
One minute there's grim grey rain, then postcard sunshine,
and next the operatic climax as heaven spills glory
in a turbulent sunset. The hotels have become rest homes;
the dead theme parks rot in dirt. In those rest homes,
the elderly sit wordlessly, staring at the sea. It moves, they don't.
Everyone else wanders uncomfortably, in a shabby stumble.
The old nuclear power station warmed the bay, brought sharks in.
They joined the shrimp and cockles sold in tubs at the cheerful
kiosks that remain like warts along the prom. My childhood
dream:
get me the fuck out of here. Please –

Recently I found a pound coin there, on the street where my ex
dropped a quid thirty years ago. I'd love to pretend that it's
the same one, but it isn't. No one even has the heart to write
proper graffiti. Oh, bring me sunshine, Eric.
I loved, hated you, town. I'm sorry. You were so ugly.
Outside my window, seagulls swore at each other and ate vomit.
We all wore cheap tat and old loved denim. They used to say,
the pier was burned down for the insurance. Twice.
There were ghosts of the coach and horses that sank
in the sucking sands. The ghosts have pissed off too,
save for the drowned cocklers, that recent trip to misery.
A biker, caught in quicksand, yelled, 'Save the bike!'
His mates did in a swift minute, then turned to find
their friend gone, just like that. Me, oh, sex on the beach
under the stars, with some bloke who didn't even like me.
It was all that there was, then.

If you walked off the main road, there were needles everywhere.
Shocked posh folk from Lancaster fled as fast as Volvos can go.
Today's headline: rich local businessman launches new enterprise
to rejuvenate the area. This is doomed to failure, always,
though not necessarily for the businessman. I fear living there
again.
All that hope and effort, and for what? Poor sods. Poor us.
They still sell postcards with 'fifties photos showing good clean
family fun, new and wholesome in the sun. I keep coming back,
in my mind, to those sunsets. You wouldn't think it'd be enough
to draw everything together, to stop a town from dying. Glory.

Calculated

Everyone takes her measure
as Candela enters the room,
her dress a nebula, airy with valences.
(Lady Calorie Langley frowns, mutters
behind her fan to her loyal Slyke.)
Candela's joules are breathtaking
– the bracelet of twinking amperes,
and at her throat, a huge, flawless erg.
At her side is Petri Faraday, Count of Volt,
drinking tola and admiring the lustre
of the coulombs in his beloved's hair.
They tread a measure in the dance:
a rundlet, an edison, a quire.
He asks after her pet picomoles,
Mips and Mutchkin, and she laughs.
(The anarchist Smoot looks on in
jealous frustration. He sees the sea-miles
in her eyes; knows she will never smile
at him.)
Supper is laid on the periodic table:
centipawns in ream sauce, charka-baked
mease, sweet poiseuilles, endless magnons
of sparkling lanac. A violinist plays
Mercalli and mournful Danfon,
who are as fashionable as silken ells,
furlong boots and polished acre.
More dancing follows, and Candela flings
herself into a wild legua.

At midnight she calls loudly for her furman
to bring round the carriage; but as she
passes Faraday, she furtively slips her cordel
into his hand. He nods very slightly,
inhaling her scent of centibar.
Tonight's moment will be lepton.
C'est la crore.

Going Beep in the Night

It woke us every midnight
with a sinister beep beep beep.
It was the sound of our printer
- the one that had died exactly
a year ago. We shivered.
What did it want?

Sometimes a light would flash.
'Paper jam,' we'd mumble
in our sleep. There was no paper.
There was no printer.

We called in our shaman: the friend
who works in IT support and knows
the mysteries of wires, lights and
chips. He stayed overnight and paled
– and he had been pale to start with.

'A digital exorcism,' he pronounced,
and oh what an unplugging and restarting
and charging of batteries for healthy
machines – and sorrowful laying to rest
and thanks for those who will go
'to the farm' for elderly hardware.

Two days later, the sounds had gone.
Either the exorcism had worked,
or the printer had run out of juice.
Our phones blink tears of light.

Not Cricket

Showers that you left, grubbier than you were before;
shivering, skidding on frozen mud;
netball, hockey, rounders and lacrosse
made it clear that you were an indoor loner
– yet never left alone, and longing for it,
and now the yoga, pilates, the Youtube demos
aren't so much for health as for solitude,
something never taught at school.

Something never taught at school: the graceful arts
of silence and creative movement,
of pen sprinting across page, hurdling
the gaps between words and lines
– telling of those long, lost, cold, crowded days,
life a bruising game played for a team you didn't support.

Ms Bryant is Dangerously Delusional
(*These statements have all been said/written about me and my partner, Keir.*)

They keep the curtains closed.
The plumber will say of the claimant's partner, 'He wouldn't let me go upstairs to check the radiators.'
Other people have found Keir Thomas to be brusque or even threatening.
We were escorted by Keir Thomas and a 'friend', who weighing between 18-20 stone was clearly intended to be intimidatory.
They always keep the curtains closed.

Catherine Bryant was (or was feigning to be) asleep.
I believe she is falsely claiming benefits.
Therefore I was justifiably angry.
I have had to give the claimant a wide berth, as her inventive malice and the belligerence of her partner causes me to feel nauseated.
The claim is fabricated. The claimant is irrational, vindictive and dangerously delusional.
If she can write a letter then she's not that disabled.
In spite of all her disabilities she was able to visit Heptonstall graveyard – to visit a grave.
You seldom see the curtains open.

These videos show her speaking readily and adjusting her clothing whilst holding a glass.
She was apparently well enough to judge a poetry competition.
She is pulling the wool over the taxpayers' eyes.
She has taken every opportunity to pursue me with an excess of vindictive communications.
She used falsehood in an attempt to justify all the fabrications and exaggerations with which she embellishes her accusations. After all, she does claim to be a 'creative writer'.

We do not dispute that Ms Bryant is disabled.
She has made an occupation of tailoring disability to her advantage.
I am probably not her first, nor her last victim.
She keeps the curtains closed.

Bite Down Hard

I know what the tooth fairy does with the teeth.
I know that a dentist once kept her prisoner
for a year and a day. He was one of those who say,
'I love you,' and then lock you in.

She threw a handful of teeth at him and sang
a spell of releasing, but it didn't work
beacause teeth aren't magic. Like bones,
they're the stones of the body and very romantic,
but for magic you need blood, hair and jewellery.

I can't tell you how she escaped in case
a dentist is reading this, but leave a request
scribbled in pencil with your next tooth,
or just hum when among honeysuckle flowers,
and the answer will come to you.

Cargo

Breasting vitreous green waves came ships
bound for Murano, with cargoes of smashed glass,
two hundred years ago.
'Recycling' is recent – 'remaking' they called it,
taking the broken to be unbroken, relaunched.
Sometimes the journey itself was fractured,
once by a storm.
The seas and skies screamed at each other;
the keel timbers shivered and wrenched apart,
painfully, offshore; and instead of being melted, remade
at the sure hands of workers,
the fragments and slivers were sent, with the crew,
by the elements to the sea and shore;
to the oceans and beaches from which they came,
to shine brokenly once again.

Bardmon K's review of 'Poem' by A. Famous-Poet

It didn't do what I wanted it to do.
He's lost it, hasn't he? Not that
he was ever as good as people reckon.
The imagery didn't work. It was too
obscure. Not that I didn't understand
it, you know – of course I did.
It was just too esoteric. Other lines
were too simple and obvious.
I prefer someone else's work.
You don't need to read examples
from the text – my mellifluous yet
edgy prose erupts onto the page,
and is all the evidence needed.
The subject has been addressed
in poetry before – there's no USP
(Unique Selling Point). At one
point he uses an adjective. That's bad!
People like him stop new, exciting
poets from exploding onto the scene.
It's too carefully constructed.
I like raw poetry. It didn't do what
I wanted it to do. He's over with, now,
right?

Falconar's Flautist

I heard it in the night, abroad
– a single ringing note, purer
than the usual breathy lisp of flutes.
It was a leaping new music,
a clapperless yet sounding bell,
direct from the soul of Apollo.

I imagined the flautist, an exotic bird,
fragrant with peach and lime feathers
forming the most luxurious tassels and trains;
or a nightingale, only brighter,
singing in shimmering ultramarine.

At dawn, as the mists took unhurried leave
and the trees began to steam in the sun,
I saw the flautist: a tiny frog
the size of my thumbnail
– a scrap of jade – a little living leaf.

I knew that this was better than the bird,
that here was show not tell.
I laughed aloud as that thought blew in.
The frog ignored me, playing on
until she had raised the whole of the sun.

Based on an incident from A.E.I. Falconar's 'Gardens of Meditation'

Fear and the Familiar

Some people are so frightened
of poetry
that if you take prose
and set it out like this,
they will smile self-deprecatingly,
claim not to understand it
and move on instantly
to the next comforting advert.

I Have Tried to Stop Eating Stars

I have tried to stop eating stars;
they make me gassy.
I know that planets should be eaten by the galaxy,
all resting on one's fork, full of fibre and crunch
and water and magma.
I know that asteroid belts, if eaten whole,
contain all the necessary elements for health,
especially if one swallows
the odd meteor shower too.
And they all say, have the occasional comet.
It does no harm.
But don't eat the stars.
Don't eat the stars!

I can't help it. I see them there
in their sweetmeat box, chosen to show
them off as much as possible, and I long
for that full mouthful of warm comfort.

The red ones, a touch overripe, are the best
– spicy, sometimes bursting on your tongue.
Afterwards I feel warm and energetic.
I can juggle gods after a few suns.

One day I'll explode with the gluttony
of warmth and light, and spew out the most
voluptuous universe, all light and curves.

Social Etiquette, 1950s

At-Homes: a smartly tailored suit
– not the tweedy variety, of course –
a two-piece outfit, or an afternoon dress
with fur coat are equally correct.
The hour for your first at-home must,
of course, be arranged to suit your husband
and his friends, and you may prefer
a cocktail party. Stand up refreshments
are the rule. Choose food easily managed
while balancing a teacup or glass.

The registrar must be notified. The nearest
relatives walk behind the coffin. Letters
of condolence are not expected except
from relatives or intimate friends.
It is correct to provide a light luncheon
or tea after the ceremony for those attending.
Widows: cap and veil should not be worn.
Lawn cuffs and collars are correct if desired.
Diamonds and pearls may be worn with deep
mourning. Black-edged paper and cards
may still be used during the mourning period,
but this custom is rapidly dying out.

Source material: 1000 Household Hints, Elizabeth Craig, 1952

Sylvia Plath Talks about England

That enunciation in a voice as deep as Cape Cod
with high waves to the feminine clouds:
like her hair, blonde yet dark.

She loved black cabs and courtesy.
'The weather infects me –'
She stops to laugh, meant 'affects'
'– but yes, it does infect me!'

Sylvia was taken in the rain through redbrick rows
of cutpaper terraces: 'undetached' houses
to the sea, the Yorkshire sea and that sea
a muddy wash where people, smothered
in plastic raincoats, littered gum wrappers underfoot,
shivered and had their holiday.

Seeing whole pigs in butchers' shops,
she felt faint. The pigs turned off and on,
now sick pink, now blanched white,
like marshmallows, though not at all like marshmallows.
But she became a convert. Relished experience.

There were hopes of Cornwall, for the kids,
when the weather was warmer. She spoke
of England as hospitable to artists, welcoming eccentricity,
cited a woman who embroidered penicillium mould
in needlepoint and offered cats as hot water bottles.

Yes, England welcomed the uncommercial,
artistic and odd, said Sylvia.
And didn't we make her stay special.

Transition

No more glühwein at the Christmas markets;
no more exquisite ice miniatures by the million.
Spring paints everything in primary colours
and tells us all to have sex all the time,
birds shrilling yelling boasting about it.
Stillness is a gentle memory to sigh at.
Nothing is silent or spare now.
Spring is rococo gone loco.

We sat at windows, hands hugging mugs
of scarlet soup as we watched sledges raced by kids
too young for Spring, though it'll get them.
Those girls fluffed up in marshmallow hats
and pink points of glove or scarf will go
on bikini diets, tormenting their pre-teen flesh.
Those boys laughing and galumphing will start
to feel lost and hurt and desperate.
The clear air will thicken and humidify.

No more the early evening snooze by a
lid-drooping fire; no more long ballgown night
easy on eyes and encouraging of long sleeps.
No more cocoa poured from saucepans
after a snow-beast is built.
No more dying quietly in your sleep, when ready.
Brace yourself for accidents, sudden losses
and the foolishness of a young brash season
given to bad taste in accessories
and a pungent perfume for every allergy.

Midnight Moments in the Mosh Pit
(The Ted Hughes Rap)

Yo thought fox
coming on like shock-jocks,
alive despite lonely clocks.
(*Oh God, it has come to this.*)

Cold body, bold body, bare,
two eyes serve moments – rare.
Wave your paws in the air
like you just don't care.

The shock-fox thinks
like a hole in the head, slinks,
winks, lags by stump and blinks:
this rap sharply, hotly stinks.

Yo thought-fox, never offstage,
taught in schools of the po-mo age,
clocks stopped, static on the page.
(*And the poem, betrayed into immobility,
comes to a stop.*)

Morphinesque

My friend's face shines, and her paint moves
long after she's swept it on to the canvas.
There's a semi-abstract tumble of her dogs
and I can hear yaps, rrrruffs and my friend's
laugh, and everything has that gleaming motion.

I'm alone with morphine and still, save for
the slow rotation of my mind, pushed by
the drug. It takes a year to go round my skull.
At the bad moment, my courgettes turn
into maggots, writhing in couscous.
I know just to eat them anyway.

The first time I was morphined, another friend
wore a lace-hemmed top to visit me at the
glaring hospital. The lace became maggots.
I screamed. What was most frightening
was that she didn't take off her top, and just
sat smiling, shiny-nosed, dressed in maggots.

Bad times, good times. I hold my friend's
painting up to my ear to hear. There's a silver
tinkling, the sound of a celesta playing.
The tune is simple, alien, gone in a phrase.
Then a chime, and the dogs barking again.
I replace the painting carefully. I am
infinitely lucky.

My friend shines like Julian of Norwich.
All shall be well and all shall be well
and all manner of thing shall be well.
Beneath the asphalt talking to concrete
in electric words, I can hear paint and skin.
I just make out the tiny maggot choir
singing psalms as they carry away the dead.

Shit People Say to Bisexuals

You're just greedy, aren't you?
So when do you think you'll make up your mind?
Are you a tourist?
When you're going out with a man, what's the difference between you and a straight?
You're straight really, aren't you?
When you're going out with a woman, what's the difference between you and a lesbian? You're gay really, aren't you?
Do you just want to fuck everybody?
Would you like a threesome? If so, does it have to be with one of each?
Which is better, sex with a man or with a woman?
I want you to come to more gay events, to make you more gay.
Why not just be straight? After all, you can choose.
Is it just desperation?
Do you just think that no man will want you, but you want to keep your options open?
Ah, I'm sorry to hear that – you can never settle down or get married, can you?
Well, everyone's bisexual, aren't they?
You're doubly damned because you could choose not to sin.
You are so lucky not to have to deal with any of the prejudices and preconceptions that we do.
You have it easiest of anyone, don't you?

Wuthering, Wuthering, Wuthering Heights

Kate Bush sang of her just as I
had imagined her: Cathy, Cathy,
at the window, shrieking
to be let in, like the wind.

I longed to be Kate, too,
wild and beautiful as she was,
just as the Cathy of whom she sang.
She gave me hope
that Cathys could create
and escape.

I just let out, now,
my inner Cathy, my inner Kate.

There Must Be Something In It

If you touch dandelions, you'll wet the bed.
Walk under a ladder and paint will fall on you.
It's good luck to be crapped on by elephants.
If the wind changes, your firstborn child will be hairy.
If you spill pepper, then you must immediately read
Alice in Wonderland.
If you find litter on the road, then you'll die a millionaire.
If you open your mouth when looking into a mirror,
the Devil will dive down your throat. This is a bad thing.
Eating bananas on Tuesdays will bring about the Apocalypse.
None of this is negotiable.

Skeleton Orchestra

Their instruments are bone too
— crafted with minute care from femurs
and fingers, or a lattice of ribs.
Violin, oboe, cornet — all yield silence
or a parched scraping sound.
Only the percussion thumps, masking
the rattling noises of the players,
like dried full pea pods;
and some of the wind section
make the hoots of ghostly owls.

That first violin is gesturing in
an exaggerated way, to draw attention
to herself; a serious bone-boy
strikes the triangle. The great
timpani is a giant hollow skull,
the piccolo a punctured sternum.
Playing is a full-time job.

Scrape, thunk, click punctuate the
silence like dropped coins, though
the whole orchestra is giving its all.
Just dust and fury, sadly, producing
very little. So, then, why do we watch,
why listen? Why do our bones
refuse to move, why can't we wake?

Witness Statement

I'm not telling you the whole story.
This is what you need to know.
I'm not telling you the whole story.

Something's hunted in the so-sweet meadow.
Screams are not always next door's TV.
This is what you need to know.

They think they know why, but not yet how.
Praying or preying. So what's god's deal?
Screams are not always next door's TV.

Running too slowly. All thoughts congeal.
I don't know which side I'm on now –
praying or preying. So what's god's deal?

Just *everyone* is a moral arbiter. Wow.
Little slither-fish wriggling in a pissy net.
I don't know which side I'm on now.

Don't make your mind up just yet.
I'm not telling *you* the whole story,
little slither-fish, wriggling in a pissy net.
I'm not telling you the whole story.

Aurora Borealis/Migraine

It begins as wintry prickles of light
with telling hints of gemstone shades.
Unsurprising – all day, brighty-bright TVs,
blaring radios and voices –
'Best chance in thirteen years.'
'We're going to the country.'
'Everyone's staying up.'

The nausea comes in a felling gut-punch,
a one-two with vertigo, but I've made it to bed
and cobbled together a silentish night
before the sweeping serenade of green and purple,
cheesy 1970s Top of the Pops effects
or the semaphore of god-like aliens,
hits.

Other half tears an envelope open.
The sound scythes my eyes.
'Oh God! Shut up!' 'Oh! Sorry!'
So everyone becomes whispery-fluttery
bird-snakes hissing sympathy:
'Such a shame you'll miss it!'
'It's the best chance in thirteen years.'
'We should really have gone to the country.'

They giggle their way outside, party-like,
to wait for what turns out to be
(while I lie feeling the worst tide start to ebb,
at last washing away the hated light,
the shingling, sparkling pain)
a no-show.

You Might as Well Fuck

I have never existed. Losing my virginity
did not hurt; there was a far-off twang,
like a song on someone else's radio
or clothes pinged from next door's line,
and then there was pleasure, that void
filled at last, at last.
Oh yes, I thought. I want I want I want
a lot more of this.

Not supposed to exist. I wanted cock in cunt
or cunt on cunt
and *screw* the relationship idea
unless it was open and meant sex on tap.
And oh, screw the mindless interrogation
called *chatting up*, the bad dialogue of *flirting*.
Longed to say, I want to fuck you, your friend too,
just for tonight. One night only.
Envied those who could cruise.

Hated myself, of course, but still followed
the imperative urge, chasing the rhythm
in which I became the universe and then exploded.
Later I saw that we're all trained to hate
ourselves anyway, so you might as well fuck.

Now my body has collapsed like a railway siding
from the century before last, thank the stars
that I sang with it, fucked with it, danced with it.

In novels and drama the closest you get
to me is the earthy best friend who's a bit shallow
and doesn't quite *get* the sensitive heroine.
We all miss out, on the unwritten art
but also on those thousands of nights
where I longed for any cock, any cunt
but didn't get them, while others lay wanting too.

Myriad dances missed, tenderness unhappened.
So much longing, mine and that of others, vanquished
 if only I'd been permitted to exist.

Still Life

He is primed and ready for love's sketches,
the gouache young Phthalo, and he scumbles
at first sight of the Lady Fauve by the lake.
She sits, calmly drinks chiaroscuro, keeping
her tempura even as Lord Turpentine umbers
clumsy compliments. To her all men are pastels.
Her palette demands more viridian fare.
To Phthalo she is monestial, and his cousin
Sienna's face falls as she sees him fall deep
into ultramarine feelings; she leaves, pointillist
and watercolour, and rushes off to acrylic.
Fauve looks up, sees Phthalo and loses all
perspective in a flash. Her colours are worked up,
her landscape washed with folly. She raises
her fan brush, but too late: evil Count Alizarin
has noticed the nude chrome of emotion,
and his cruel revenge will be vermillion
and representative.

Take Five Decades

The men of the generation
that actually liked jazz
and intellected about it
at apprehensive nodding girls
are all dying off now, obituaried
by their dwindling band of peers
sighing for the joys of cynicism, youth
and hard drinking. They were once felt
to be the new measure of all things
with their biting cleverness and wit.

They're replaced by my lot,
the dreary left-wingers still trying
to be nice to people and to read
as much as possible. Our tastes run to
folk hippy glam punk disco reggae
metal goth soul new romantic pop rock
– and we wish we could like rap and hip-hop.

And so dies jazz, unmourned,
from early trad to big band bland,
freeform and experimental;
and a generation of angry males,
literary lions in tweed and twill,
are reviewed away into history, and
what (*yeah*!) – what will the young
rappers write about us in thirty years,
when we die, huge and silent
on stilled turntables?

Such Life and Brilliance
from an interview with Elizabeth Taylor in Harper's Bazaar

I have never wanted to be a queen.

I never planned to acquire a lot of jewels
or a lot of husbands.

The Krupp is an extraordinary stone.
It has such life and brilliance
when light shines through it.

I am the temporary custodian.

The real Cleopatra had an incredibly complicated life
and she had to be very, very canny
to survive as long as she did.

I always wanted to be able
to connect with people in other ways
than through film.

The things that are important to me
were borne out of great passion.

Richard – we would be married again,
but it's not up for discussion.

I have known great love.

We know too much about our idols
and that spoils the dream.

I have never wanted to be a queen.

Warmer Places

'When the purple goes from the hills,'
says my neighbour,
'Then Autumn's come.'
For a moment I revel in a vision
of the heather uprooting, migrating south
for the Winter, flying in formation
and uttering little Emily Dickinson cries.
I relay the image to my neighbour
and she gives me That Look,
as if I might be serious, tourist-silly;
then her eye catches mine at the right angle
and we laugh ourselves into a new season
and a warmer place.

Bloddeuwedd's Trinity

The owls are the only celebrants
at the church now, hooting their hymns.
They offer grisly pellets at the altar
– there are no church mice left.

Three masks of barn owls
peer from a dark window,
ringed by pale stonework.
Through the quatrefoil
they watch and listen.

In feather-perfect formation,
the ternion flies to find
a world beyond the church window.

In the graveyard, a thousand flowers
blanket the dead with vivid life
– enough to make a renewed goddess laugh,
enough for an old god to yield forgiveness.

Such a Thing, My Leaping, Dancing Heart

I'd expected the ECG machine
with its beep beep beep beep
but not the scan monitor
on which my heart leaps and dances
as I haven't for thirty years.

From one angle –
(the nurse moves her hand
from here to there.
She frowns minutely,
then gets the shot)
it really is heart-shaped

– but mostly it's pure energy,
a fist of pumping muscle,
though it looks to me as if a colony
of moths has set up in it,
or hattifatteners
on some tiny electric journey.

I turn my head to share this
with my husband and see him
flooded out with tears –
'Such a thing to see
your lover's heart beating,'
he says. 'So miraculous
– such a thing.'
– which makes me liquefy too,
save for my solid, dancing heart,

which leaps. Which leaps. Which leaps.

ABOUT THE AUTHOR

Cathy Bryant worked as a life model, civil servant and childminder before writing as a profession. She has won 27 literary awards and contests, including the Wergle Flomp Humorous Poetry Contest and the Bulwer-Lytton Fiction Contest, and she has had over 250 poems and stories published. Cathy co-edited the anthologies *Best of Manchester Poets* vols. 1, 2 and 3 and has had two books of poetry published:
Contains Strong Language and Scenes of a Sexual Nature, and *Look at All the Women,* plus a nonfiction book: *How to Win Writing Competitions.*
Cathy is also responsible for the listings website for cash-strapped writers www.compsandcalls.com
Poems first published:
Erratics and *Flyleaves* in Contemporary Verse 2
Material in The Sunlight Press
Songs of the Starcleaners in Balticon 49
Circus and *Ms Bryant is Dangerous and Delusional* in *Stairs and Whispers,* Nine Arches Press 2017
The Huge Paws of Country Fog in The Scarlet Leaf Review
As Dark Asda in Star Line Daffodils was first published in Eye to the Telescope
Seeing the Glass in Antarctica Journal
January Joggers in WaxPoetryArt
Secret Knowledge in Prole
Calculated The Science Fiction and Fantasy Poetry Association
Fear and the Familiar in The Curly Mind
I Have Tried to Stop Eating Stars on www.polutexni.com
Social Etiquette, 1950s in Stirred Feminist Collective
Wuthering, Wuthering, Wuthering Heights and *Such Life and Brilliance* in Silver Birch
There Must be Something In It in The American Poetry Journal
Such a Thing, My Leaping, Dancing Heart in Wordrunner Chapbooks

MORE FROM ARACHNE PRESS
www.arachnepress.com

BOOKS

Short Stories
London Lies
ISBN: 978-1-909208-00-1
Our first Liars' League showcase, featuring unlikely tales set in London.
Stations: Short Stories Inspired by the Overground Line
ISBN: 978-1-909208-01-8
A story for every station from New Cross, Crystal Palace, and West Croydon at the Southern extremes of the East London branch of the Overground line, all the way to Highbury & Islington.
Lovers' Lies
ISBN: 978-1-909208-02-5
Our second collaboration with Liars' League, bringing the freshness, wit, imagination and passion of their authors to stories of love.
Weird Lies
ISBN: 978-1-909208-10-0
WINNER of the Saboteur2014 Best Anthology Award: our third Liars' League collaboration – more than twenty stories varying in style from tales not out of place in *One Thousand and One Nights* to the completely bemusing.
Solstice Shorts: Sixteen Stories about Time
ISBN: 978-1-909208-23-0
Winning stories from the first *Solstice Shorts Festival* competition together with a story from each of the competition judges.
Mosaic of Air by Cherry Potts
ISBN: 978-1-909208-03-2
Sixteen short stories from a lesbian perspective.
Liberty Tales, Stories & Poems Inspired by Magna Carta
ISBN: 978-1-909208-31-5
Because freedom is never out of fashion.

Shortest Day, Longest Night
ISBN: 978-1-909208-28-5
Stories and poems from the *Solstice Shorts Festival* 2015 and 2016.
Happy Ending NOT Guaranteed by Liam Hogan
ISBN: 978-1-909208-36-0
Deliciously twisted fantasy stories.
Dusk
ISBN: 978-1-909208-54-4
Stories and Poems from the *Solstice Shorts Festival 2017*

Poetry
The Other Side of Sleep: Narrative Poems
ISBN: 978-1-909208-18-6
Long, narrative poems by contemporary voices, including Inua Elams, Brian Johnstone, and Kate Foley, whose title poem for the anthology was the winner of the 2014 *Second Light* Long Poem competition.
The Don't Touch Garden by Kate Foley
ISBN: 978-1-909208-19-3 (also available as an audio book)
A complex autobiographical collection of poems of adoption and identity, from award-winning poet Kate Foley.
With Paper for Feet by Jennifer A McGowan
ISBN: 978-1-909208-35-3
Poetry exploring myth and folklore.
Foraging by Joy Howard
ISBN: 978-1-909208-39-1
Poems of nature, human nature and grief, time and memory.
A Gift of Rivers by Kate Foley (April 2018)
ISBN: 978-1-909208-53-7
Poems of migration and sexual identity.

Photography
Outcome: LGBT Portraits by Tom Dingley
ISBN: 978-1-909208-26-1
80 full colour photographic portraits of LGBT people with the attributes of their daily life – and a photograph of themselves as a child. @OutcomeLGBT

Novels

The Dowry Blade by Cherry Potts
ISBN: 979-1-909208-20-9
When nomad Brede finds a wounded mercenary and the Dowry Blade, she is set on a journey of revenge, love, and loss.

For Older Children

Devilskein & Dearlove by Alex Smith
ISBN: 978-1-909208-15-5
NOMINATED FOR THE 2015 CILIP CARNEGIE MEDAL.
A young adult novel set in South Africa. Young Erin Dearlove has lost everything, and is living in a run-down apartment block in Cape Town. Then she has tea with Mr Devilskein, the demon who lives on the top floor, and opens a door into another world.

By Ghillian Potts

Brat: Book One of The Naming of Brook Storyteller
ISBN: 978-1-909208-41-4
On her twelfth birthday Brat's father disappears. She waits, but he never comes back.

Spellbinder: Book Two of The Naming of Brook Storyteller
ISBN: 978-1-909208-46-9
Brook is abducted and forced to call the Elder Dragons to save Storyteller children held hostage, but she cannot control the dragons.

Wolftalker: Book Three of The Naming of Brook Storyteller
ISBN: 978-1-909208-49-0 (June 2018)
Someone is felling gilden trees, and the life of the Overlord is threatened.

For Younger Children

The Old Woman From Friuli
by Ghillian Potts, illustrated by Ed Boxall
ISBN: 978-1-909208-40-7
The Duke owns everything he can see from the tower of his castle, everything except a small house, a little garden and a tiny field. They belong to the old woman from Friuli, and she isn't selling.

All our books (except poetry books) are also available as e-books.